# THE SHORES OF VAIKUS

Born in Cornwall, son of an Estonian wartime refugee, **Philip Gross** has lived in Plymouth, Bristol and South Wales, where he was Professor of Creative Writing at Glamorgan University (USW). His 28th collection *The Shores of Vaikus* (2024) follows twelve previous books with Bloodaxe, including *The Thirteenth Angel* (2022), a Poetry Book Society Recommendation shortlisted for the T.S. Eliot Prize; *Between the Islands* (2020); *A Bright Acoustic* (2017); *Love Songs of Carbon* (2015), winner of the Roland Mathias Poetry Award and a Poetry Book Society Recommendation; *Deep Field* (2011), a Poetry Book Society Recommendation; *The Water Table* (2009), winner of the T.S. Eliot Prize; and *Changes of Address: Poems 1980-1998* (2001), his selection from earlier books including *The Ice Factory, Cat's Whisker, The Son of the Duke of Nowhere, I.D.* and *The Wasting Game*. Since *The Air Mines of Mistila* (with Sylvia Kantaris, Bloodaxe Books, 1988), he has been a keen collaborator, most recently with artist Valerie Coffin Price on *A Fold in the River* (2015) and with poet Lesley Saunders on *A Part of the Main* (2018). *I Spy Pinhole Eye* (2009), with photographer Simon Denison, won the Wales Book of the Year Award 2010. He received a Cholmondeley Award in 2017.

His poetry for children includes *Manifold Manor, The All-Nite Café* (winner of the Signal Award 1994), *Scratch City* and *Off Road To Everywhere* (winner of the CLPE Award 2011) and the poetry-science collection *Dark Sky Park* (2018).

PHILIP GROSS

# The Shores of Vaikus

BLOODAXE BOOKS

ISBN: 978 1 78037 717 9

First published 2024 by
Bloodaxe Books Ltd,
Eastburn,
South Park,
Hexham,
Northumberland NE46 1BS.

**www.bloodaxebooks.com**
For further information about Bloodaxe titles
please visit our website and join our mailing list
or write to the above address for a catalogue.

Cover design: Neil Astley & Pamela Robertson-Pearce.

Printed in Great Britain by Bell & Bain Limited, Glasgow, Scotland, on
acid-free paper sourced from mills with FSC chain of custody certification.

*for Juhan Karl Gross*

(1919-2011)

su südamepuuris on vaikus
ja tuhandeaastane lind
ta oskab aga ei räägi
sest ta armastab sind

JUHAN VIIDING

in the cage of your heart there is silence
and a thousand-year-old bird
it can speak however it loves you
so it never says a word.

trans. Tuulelaeval Valgusest On Aerud
(*Windship with Oars of Light*), Huma, 2001

***Vaikus:*** *one of the several words for silence in Estonian*
***Vaikimine:*** *ditto, in the sense of 'holding one's peace'*

## ACKNOWLEDGEMENTS

Acknowledgements are due to the editors of the following publications in which some of these poems first appeared: *Axon: Creative Explorations, The High Window, One Hand Clapping, Poetry Ireland Review* and *The Poetry Review*.

The frontispiece to *Evi and the Devil* on page 28 is by Reti Saks: *Leafeye*, vernis mou 2019 (etching) 40 x 24.5cm. https://www.reti.ee/

# CONTENTS

*With thanks to Andres, Doris, Miriam*
*and other friends in Estonia*

*...not silence, so much as*

*the larger voice*

*of things...*

# TRANSLATING SILENCE

## The Old Country

Not far, and not near,
scarcely sound, more a hitch
in the hush that insists
        until I stop my breath and listen...
        Something like a long-held breath
        released, small and distinct, particular.

The storm moved over last night
letting the sea down again, that Baltic flatness
slightly darkened, with a battered look,
        while here in the summer house garden
        May sun is teasing up wisps from the eaves
        and from the cut ends in a log pile

so perfectly end-stopped,
with such understanding of each log's different
place together, that a night of storm
        is nothing but steam rising –
        that and the honey-tart tang of pine sap
        reawakening, and that sound

which is this year's new wasp
bent to its diligence, scraping a track in the wood,
straight, pale, already digesting
        to paper spit pulp, to nest, to layers
        of inwardness, chamber into chamber, word of mouth,
        recollecting itself. Almost weightless.

So little can stand for so much: that
sound for log pile, for resin smell, for then, for morning
after, for that old small country. Close my eyes
        from the sun, and there's the woodshed
        in blue shadow, as if the storm had kept on coming
        and this low and level only-just-a-land

was seabed again – all this, clear,
framed, as a deep-dive camera's eye
might catch a hundred-year-old wreck
    beneath the ice. Inside the porthole,
    tables laid. There might be music playing
    if we could be still enough to hear.

## Introits

Inside the empty cartridge case:
a bird flock scattering for ever from a point
where past and future are impacted; time there never moves again.

Inside the forest: an unravelment
of paths through the same darkness – convergences too
but they are only meeting to remind each other no two are the same.

Inside the empty house, door skewed
on a hinge, a family of silences have settled, bickering
now and then the way families do. You can knock but they won't hear.

Inside the old woman's eye
is a small night, just distance enough for the lens
to creak into focus on a retina as pitted as the surface of the moon.

Inside the night outside the window –
yes, even the outside has an inside of its own –
dim intricate creatures, weaving their cocoon around our history.

Inside the taut whorl of the river's eddy
where a boulder breaks it: a strand of the moon, spun
to fine wire, strong enough for the garroting of a careless passer-by.

Inside the sound of leaves and wires:
their rough translations of the wind – poor wind,
it has no voice of its own – a hundred synonyms for *far, far, far*.

Inside the gnat swarm, one who's sure
he's grasped the higher pattern of their dance;
he'll vouchsafe the secret if you let him whisper it deep in your ear.

Inside the days where I live are others
where I never was or will be. If I speak to them
they answer me by name. As if they know me through and through.

Inside the word, this word or the next
you can think, the scuff and scratch of human voices
just out of reach. Inside here: elsewhere. Inside elsewhere: here.

## A Place Called Vaikus

The question isn't where
so much as how to say it. Say:
  like sinking into a pool
  of peat-brown water in a marsh

from one horizon to the other
only linked by the seep-seep
  stitching of whimbrel in flight.
  Down here it's dark

until the mud you've stirred up
settles
  round a glint, a word

passed in a language you don't understand
between the sunlight
  in the other world
  that of continually changing

and a bronze axe
thrown into forever
  only yesterday
  four thousand years ago.

*

Its song... Pärt's *Spiegel im Spiegel,*
a deliberation of raindrops
from the eaves

of a house you will no longer
find on any street,

a fire still embers
not cold in the empty room,

a solitude surely

though whose it is
it's not my place to say.

*

Its stories. There are red-capped mushrooms
to and fro between the trees
like drops of blood marking a path.
                The kind of story

in which a child might find a windmill
in the deepest thicket, its sails
tangled in the branches,
                yet when he turns away,

the sound of grinding from within.

Its stories and its sense. He smiles
to himself, the child –
he's read that kind of story,
                oh, for centuries.

He walks on.

*

Unforgettable

the memories
you never had

and yet
and yet

*

What to do, though, with the other
countries, which are this one, preserved
in every shade of amber, through
from lucent birch sap to blood-garnet,
from fond sunset to smoke-drapes under-lit by fire?

Depthlessly thin, rarely catching the light,
they stand around, among, between us,
not only the ones leaned at all angles
to our longing in deep forest, or offshore,
adrift and at home among the mirage islands;

also in mirror-glass downtown. Cool,
moon-bluish, a nuance of sunlight from ten
storeys up (Swedbank...the Radisson Hotel...)
falls on a clinker-built house as stranded
as a boat on shingle, and on you,

looking up as if bewitched, you, soundless
as on a web cam. Other countries...
All around you, present absences:
those exiles who never returned

but went on building, back, back, each
their own Estonia... You might be full-face,
in your blurry moment, on a live feed to the dead.

*

Country knowing itself by flickers
coding news from off the edge
of sight or hearing – thus
                    the internet,
the first swallows' return,
the first shiver that clumps them
        on the wires, or fills
the goose-flock with unsettlement
like sails unhitched from too-
long furling to face north.
                    Or the stir

in the gunmetal heart of neighbours
brooding on the brittleness
of empires, how their fractured
                    edges can be honed
to lacerate. That we are in the grip
of larger shifts and flows than us
is no surprise. From time to time
                    the time comes
                              and we know.

## Erratics

The long day's warmth, still held this longer
evening in the body of the pink-bronze
granite – stray boulder that rode
the ice train down
from Finland
and now stands
waist-deep in tideless Baltic –
you could wade to it – ten thousand
year old child on the platform gazing home.

*

It was the stillness stopped me, stillness which is anything
but static: slow, wide, bay-wide swell too slight

to notice, almost, but for up-ripples of light
the evening sun takes from its lift and dip

translated to the different-angled face of each
stone, cooling but look, melting upwards – boulders

as unsure as I am of the down or up of things
reflected. Floating on the surface, on recumbent sky.

*

In its heart, it's a lake,

this sea; a thousand-mile melt pool,
more a memory of the imperially creaking
edifice of ice than a wish to be seen.

You could mistake this calm for innocence,
holding the light on its upturned palms,
its wave-mass no more than a shrug,

but look at the ship's-mast pines
laid out flat in a track from the flayed
foreshore straight across the peninsula,

the windthrow, spreading the warp for the weft;
or closer, at a felled trunk almost feathery
with rot – how things come apart,

letting go of their shapes,
with lichen, mould, ant-fidget fizzing,
each at its own rate, digesting the waste;

look at the village churchyard, equally
windthrown, the names you half know
on the headstones of the drowned.

*

*Kivikülv: stonefield.*
strewn through the forest,
a sowing of stones...
As yet, none has grown,

but the seasons are long,
the ice-gardener indifferent
to the difference between centuries,
or sea from land from sea.

*

On terminal moraine each granite has, or is,
a fingerprint –
some pink, with big sugary flakes of feldspars;
                    some greyish, introspective, dense.

Or here, a waist-high lump of mica schist,
a night-sky-dumpling, its thousand stars
glittering on, off, as you walk around it.

Each, like an accent, is a message you can read,
about an elsewhere.
The particular parish where it was grubbed up,
                    the glacier's gigantically abraded grit.

This moves us, naturally. Erratics, wanderers...
But then, all granite is in exile. Imagine the grief
of magma, expelled from the Earth's core.

*

No wonder they are named, the greatest boulders.

Even the stray ones, away from the track, with only numbers –
          you become aware of them, like grey beasts,

something older than the elk (which also is returning)
          with their heavy-shouldered hunch, keeping low

as they graze among the start-ups of young green,

the would-be spruces in among the vertiginous thrust
          of the pines. Peaceful creatures, not

concerned with us, who in their timescale
          are as flimsy, glittery, as flies,

they nudge through clearings white-lit from beneath
by frost-corals of moss... Solitaries:

*Metsamunk*, the Forest Monk, the Hermit...

You might, if you've troubled to come so far,
consult one. Absorb its long licheny stare.

Sit, sit till night falls and the counsel you had hoped for
has gone without saying. Your bones

hear it. Stone's voice. Language they both understand.

*

A cuckoo calls, once,
in the endlessly-faceted hall
of pine trunks
and is everywhere.

## The Point

An hour beyond the stonefield, something changes. On both sides, in stray squints of distance between tree trunks, the first glints of sea. One more turn in the path; then sea and sky are almost all around us. Palganeem. The furthest point.

You can't help counting out the lastnesses. The last building, a crumbling, though barely forty-year-old, Soviet watch post, where searchlights tracked the westward shoreline, half a century... It is already archaeology. The only notice, in Estonian – *Danger of collapse. Remain here on your own responsibility.* You have a choice.

Huge beautiful surreal graffiti blossoms deep inside the tower. It seems to endorse the warning, seems to enjoy the paradox... At the hollow upstairs window, a bearded, ponytailed young man sits swinging his legs, his attention way beyond us, gazing out to sea.

Lastnesses... On the last beach – of stones ground down by ice and sea to granite boules, from tennis ball to football size, each step a little treadmill – the last tree, singular and... I almost said *frail.* Nothing frail could be here. To be one of the forest-mass, that's easy, but this...?

The last boulders – you can trace them, heads just above water, for a long way out. The last island, flat as an inking in of the horizon line, beyond.

To go, to turn back, or to stay forever. You have, you always have, a choice.

## The Crossing

Behind the boat, a shimmer-smeech of diesel,
briefly. The sea unmarked by wake. Already

it's been almost always we have been half way –

the coast, with the gull-speckled nick of the dock
behind, getting farther... Islands, never closer

and flat as the map smoothed on a plan chest
they'd seemed from a mile above.

Recently risen, with their memory of being seabed
still drying out slowly in cool northern sun –

six thousand years is nothing – now
that they've acquired a taste for rising, rising still,

the way they float up, off the grey-blue-
against-blue-grey sea horizon on the mirage;

how they part along the seam, quite gently,

like a dotted line between the real and the unreal,
with an instruction: tear here.

# EVI AND THE DEVIL

***When I was small***, I ran into the forest. No one came to find me. I lay in a heap of pine needles. Maybe the ants consumed me, I can't tell. My parents still don't know a thing about this. As far as they know, what walked out of the forest, what sat down with her dolls by the sand pit, was a little girl.

*

***I found an old pipe*** in the forest. In it, pine needles and ashes, humus, and some very tiny bones. Like an owl pellet but burned. After that I heard it calling some nights, deep in the wood: the fire owl. Some mornings we found there had been another of those unexplained house fires in the night.

*

***The kind man*** from the Youth League gave me the toy soldiers. He whittled them himself, with his beautiful knife. I think he noticed that whenever a game was being got together I wouldn't be there. I stood them on the old tin tray, then made it make a sound like far off thunder. Then they all marched one way. They fell one by one, till they were a river of logs. One last man wading.

*

***There's a small lake*** of silence – OK, I mean a large pool, really – in the heart of the woods. I thought everyone knew that, but gradually I realised that none of my classmates did. Not the rough ones, who would punch me, nor the smart ones, who knew better ways than that. Imagine the thrill: to lure them to a picnic in the forest, then to see their faces stiffen as they looked into the water. Then to pour them a glass of it each, so no one could tell, or know there was a thing to tell, not even to themselves.

*

***Thin-blooded***, my grandfather slept on the stove. I used to wonder at the energy with which my father stoked it. I understand that better now. He wanted to dry him out completely, to a stick figure we could keep propped in the window making a rude gesture – you know that fearless scorn the old are blessed with – to frighten the Devil away.

*

***There are more people*** living in the village. Yet the more there are, the emptier it feels. The more rustling with life the forest. Or maybe it's the forest dwellers coming in to live amongst us, in their thin disguises. Crane Beak Woman, for instance – I've seen how she looks at Frog Feet Man. I don't remember when I was told that I wasn't to mention these things, or by whom.

*

***I ran through the forest*** as fast as I could. I ran in a straight line, no ducking or weaving. The trees would dance out of the way. Then stepped back just in time to trip or catch a whack to anyone pursuing me. My brother broke his head like that on more than one occasion. Not that anyone believed me.

*

***You know those sudden round clearings*** in the forest? That's where the Devil squats, grandly, to fart. Things wither. It's because he can't resist the mushrooms. He asks the country people which are good to eat, and we tell him the bad ones. In the end, given time, he moves on. We build in the clearings. But you have to let the air clear first. This isn't a story, this is history.

*

***In a corner of the woods*** lives the Glass Man. I'm almost sure I've seen him now and then – sometimes a slight quirk in the field of vision, sometimes a thin prismatic glint like the edge of a mirror. Once, I think, he was just like us – opaque, corporeal – but completely consumed by his job, which strained out all the slight impurities that impede the flow of light.

*

***The trees won't speak to me***. Or to each other, though somehow they have agreed on the subject of me. That's what a forest is, its kind of silence. A conspiracy of solitudes.

*

***Some days the mist*** lifts just a few feet from the marshes. It hangs around head height, so you'd need to climb a tree to see over, just there where there are none. Or you have to crouch down, wriggle skew-kneed, to see under. Which suddenly grants you the knowledge possessed by the toad beneath its stone.

*

***The river appears*** where it wants to, going this way or that through the woods. It brings its whiff of moss and dark things, so that one or two days later you can still smell where it has been. No laws can explain this, so why try? All I know is that if you were to go with it, follow as it cuts a cleft down between stones, the place it goes to might not be the sea. It might be inland, deeper, where if anyone has been, they haven't come back to tell.

*

***Thank you, measles***, or was it mumps, whatever – my first guide into that world that sits inside and yet is larger than our own. I felt my body round me, clogged with wrongness, like a city flooded knee deep, no one should have built there but they cope. The weeks of mud and struggle after, just to move or be. I saw myself moving through it, curious and not afraid to stare. I saw how many other people lived there. Old Mrs Groanma next door. Several uncles. We passed each other, measles leading me from day to street to week to doorway, free from explanation or politeness. We passed and glanced and nodded, enough said.

*

***I was born old***, to young parents. Trouble was, they kept on ageing, while I had to hurry up and grow down so I could pass myself off as their child. So we crossed paths in the forest, and waved, and went on. By the time these words reach you I might already be too young to remember what they used to mean.

*

***I had my babies early***. In my mother's womb. But, how not to get caught? I concealed them inside me, and their children's children too, in concentric layers. Then I was born, with my innocent but private smile. The one I still have, when my mother asks me those endless questions that can never quite say 'family?'

*

***Come out of the sauna shack, uncle***, I remember everybody shouting. In the end the whole family stood around it, wondering which of the grownups would barge down the door. I still feel it's my fault that I ran straight over and unlatched it, and there he was gone. Dissolved completely, just a puff of uncle-scented steam.

*

***Who doesn't keep bees*** in this village? They're easy to love. There's the honey, of course, and more, the general hum of homing. Me, I'm with the wasps – the way they lick-scrape wood paste from your garden chair, then off with it to build the lovely hollow planet of their nest. I love the faint hieroglyphics they leave. Decipher those, we might know all we need to know about the world.

*

***I caught sight of four swans*** in a straight flight, low and unswerving, up along the course of an almost invisible stream. One glimpse, then a flicker of them behind the trees, then not that. But the damage was done. I was relative. Whatever reason I'd had setting out from home ten minutes earlier was vague, indeterminate, gone.

*

***The oldest person in the village*** is young Aare's baby. Nothing shocks him. He has seen it all before. For a few weeks he would bestow the blue mist of his gaze on each man who went by, as if he might identify his father. It wasn't till the swans passed over, northbound, that he clapped, laughed, called, and then wept as their sound faded, and from then on he was truly one of us.

*

***The Devil is a postman***. Comes round with his sack of letters from the whole wide world, his world, he says, with their pretty duplicitous stamps. It's probably true – it is his world – but he lies anyway, because he likes to. Everybody needs a hobby. See him licking his little translucent sticky hinges, arranging the lies, the pretty ones and the important-looking ones, on the squared pages in his album.

*

***It's been no time at all,*** geologically speaking, since this was a sea bed. That's still where I go to sleep some nights. Down in the kelp forest. I should stay there really – better for everyone – but my nerve fails, so I stomp my feet in the silt, till it swirls, and what the world calls history begins to rise.

*

***First it was the raiders*** landing in their thin boats, with their hungry disposition. Later we used to line the shores ourselves, wondering if where the hungry ones came from was better than here. Then the authorities came up with it, their kind of answer: they abolished the shore. Look for it now, all you come to is reed beds, no definite edge. We hissed, like the reeds, but learned to live with it.

*

***We had some terribly blond people once***, coming through here with ideals and uniforms, and a loathing of darkness. The blonder they got, the darker the shadows behind them. So it goes. What hope is there, with such a snug equation?

*

***The sea froze***. It got so cold so fast that rows of foam fret stopped in mid curl, without falling. From a high tree I saw shipwrecks, people just abandoning their small boats, overboard and hanging in the ice froth. At first I thought that it would save them but no, it only meant that they'd be always drowning, never drowned.

*

***Bloodberries***, in their season. Spot after spot. You follow their trail deeper into the wood. The flattened underbrush. Can't rest without knowing, and at the same time know that if you find what made it you might never rest again.

*

***Everyone died***. I went into the woods one morning, in a huff about something, something over breakfast. When I came back there they were, all the bodies laid out in a line. The house ripped open and everything gone. I started to retell the story as quick as I could, so they all came back, mama, papa, Timo, and my whole class from school, which was good of me, you must agree. Only, nothing they said to each other sounded quite the same, and when I looked away, they said nothing at all.

*

***Bones make good foundations***, said the old man. There seemed to be no malice in his voice. See that lighthouse, he said, see that gun emplacement? Me or my grandfathers, we built that, and that. See this island? Limestone, ground up shells and bones. I wouldn't wonder my folks had a hand in that too.

*

***Every now and then I broke a teacher.*** No harm meant, you understand. They were too shrill, too brittle, they might shatter, splinters everywhere, people had to be warned. And they made it so easy, that's an insult in itself. Take Mrs Tamm. All I did was pay attention, like she told us to. Not blinking. Three minutes of that, she couldn't look away. Then I'd take my gaze very slightly away, just over her shoulder, till she started twitching, couldn't help herself, she had to look. Then everybody was looking. Just behind her. Always. She broke. Mind you, all the grownups felt like that in those days. Don't look but...behind you. Sometimes it was true.

*

***It's not true*** that they made the masts of sailing boats from pine trees. It's the other way around. All those centuries of sailships that must have been lost in these waters, think... There might have been a sand bank. And when enough of them were piled together, mud settled round them, then the moss and mushrooms came. Then birds. Worms. Those masts put out leaves and grew.

*

***You say this is childish***. Childish, you say, to pretend this way to childhood when in reality I'm sitting on one of the lower overhanging branches of the tree of knowledge, swinging my bare legs, laughing,

*

***A hermit*** built his little cell not far from here. Good man, he was, so good. The Devil, though, he camped outside, waiting for a word with him. No joy. So the Devil had a plan. He sat by the drainpipe, where the hermit flushed his toilet; when it came, all full of stale prayers, the Devil made a wind. Wafted it over the village, so everything festered and stank. At last the people of the village came out and complained. Oh God, the hermit wailed, what have I done? So he walled up the drainpipe from the inside and, well, you can imagine it. That was the end of him, and what a way to go.

*

***You say I'm going on a bit*** about the Devil. There are angels out there too, playing their grave boys' games in the forest. Sometimes you find small heaps of pinecones stacked like fossil hand grenades.

I found one of those too, from the war. No, I won't tell you where I hid it. I might need it one day.

*

***Every word my parents did not say*** became me, one more hollowed-out space, just the shape of the not-word. Any sound of wind, leaf-murmur, scuffle on the undergrowth would resonate precisely, without my even knowing, with the timbre of what had been unsaid.

*

***You say it's the edge of the world*** but we are well connected. Traders came here to find amber for Byzantium, Barbary corsairs, the souk of Baghdad. The emperor Nero had a monocle of amber – it made him feel like a sun god, shining on his world. And sometimes like the small boy deep in the woods who pokes another ant into the sticky resin and watches it drown in slow motion, in time. Another gift of mine, he's thinking, to posterity.

*

***One day I built Venice*** in a corner of the forest. It seemed called for, a mouldering palazzo or two, something groggy with malaria and grandeur, less than steady on its feet. Glints of murder, a matter of course. And sticky threads of all the appetites that bind the known world. As Doge I elected this spider. Embassies, argosies, Marco Polo must set out again. Lost on the silk road, straying northwards. Ice and snow. Here he comes now, though a forest no Venetian can conceive of, to a clearing, where he will discover... me.

*

***The Devil cornered me*** as I was on my way home, out too late. *Ha-hah!* he said, and *Hah!* in case I missed it first time. *You know what devils do with juicy little girls like you*. I do, I said, Aunt Katri told me. *What?* he said. *Eat us*, I said. *Ho-hoh! Worse than* *that. We slobber all over you while we do it.* Uh-huh. She said that too. He leaned very close up. *Even in your inmost creases,* he breathed in my ear. Uh-huh. *She said that too?* Oh yes, you and Aunt Katri, you agree about everything. You ought to get married. *Hrruh!* he snorted, but he went off through the woods in her direction, carefully brushing his tail.

*

***There used to be a poet***, had a summerhouse outside the village. Sometimes I would catch him striding, crashing through the woods. Da DUM da DUMdum DA, he'd be intoning, building great girdered stanza cages for the stuff. That's when I learned to love words. I'd see them scattering, fleeing though the undergrowth in front of him. I helped them go to ground, where they belong.

*

***Thank you, silence***, for this clean straight edge around me – this dimension, and this one, and this. It makes a container, a cube more crystalline than I could fashion, to freeze an ice-cube inch of this, and this, and this.

*

***Crane Beak Woman***, it was years before I dared come close enough to see. I saw why you pecked so, jabbed and jabbed with that cruel beak. I saw your clipped wing feathers. Who had done that to you, and how long ago?

*

***They found the Glass Man*** shattered. No clues, no one or everyone accused. Nobody asked me, but I knew the whole scene could be reconstructed – just measure the angles at which we found them embedded in everybody else, those needle-thin splinters of glass.

*

***Grandmother muttered incantations***. Words whose meaning escaped her. Curses maybe. Assuredly things went to hell. Teach me, I wanted to say. But she couldn't. The words had drawn back underneath their surface, snake beneath a stone, with all the power of what can't be touched or understood.

*

***Of all the forest-comers*** could there be an Ant Man? Are you crazy? Imagine it, the spirit of an ant. A single ant, that is. One boy in my class, he has to be an ant hill, shedding himself on all sides, wasting and not caring, trickling, sprawling, turning up inside your knickers and your creases. Grub him out, and he's already somewhere else, inheriting the earth.

*

***I don't need to have a shape*** or surface. Trust the rain, that fine damp prickling in the air. It moulds me, if I stand still. Stops at just the right distance from the warm core of me. Merely indicates the casually negotiated edge which we shall call, for want of better words, a face.

*

***My little ferretchild***, feral mudscuffler... Him, with his spyglass and his spats and his scholarly manner, he thought he could make a pet of me. Naturalist, my arse. I was something he'd let slip, he thought, half a lifetime ago. So be it. I led him deep into the forest, turned him twice about, and vanished. Maybe the real wild things got him, I didn't go back to check. And if they did, could that be what he wanted all along?

*

***The wind bows the trees down***, sweeping, a forest of brooms in a rage. They are trying to sweep up everything, especially themselves. Like a mad janitor whose dream is to stand at last alone, in a room as steely clean and empty as... We have no words to say what.

Maybe as the sky, the sea.

*

***The island is a flat stone*** skimmed across the water. Very slowly. Very. Resting now in contact, on a give or take of surface tension, but wait for centuries to come: we'll lift again and hang before the next skid-whack of impact in midair.

*

***They say a piece of the sky*** once fell here. A crumb flicked off your heedless God's lapel. I'd have liked to see that moment of astonished hush, as the sea boiled off, then crashed back. Some days I trip over a vaporised nothing. Or look up, where the air was ruptured. See straight through the duplicitous blue.

*

***A blackened log*** came up out of the peat-soup pool, with the face of a hacked god. Terminally sad moustaches. Dripping. Somebody's mother was calling Come home (in her bog-voice) your tea's getting cold, so I pushed him back in.

*

***Wind blows***, the rain comes over and people with it, blowing west out of chill steppe, blowing east again. They're like us, these shapes in the rain, but grey-faced, bent at the wind's angle. They pass through us and among us, rain through mist. Yes, to them we're mist people, rising from the damp earth, fading. Never quite there when they speak. One substance, them, us, water mainly, but how to grasp each other, ours, the language of mist's eternal afterthought, theirs, the language of the driven rain?

*

***Clear the trees***, I've heard them saying, then we'll get a clear sight of the island. Things will make sense. I can tell them what they'll find that day, when it's too late: that the place is a raft, barely floating, made of the roots and the constant fall of branches – and sinking, from that moment on.

*

***They built a road through the forest***, dead straight. We knew the trees went on forever. Now they were forever on that side, and again on this. All of a sudden, two infinities.

*

***Did I say virgin*** pinewood? A camp of boys on distant postings. A village nearby. Half the kids in my school had glints of somewhere distant in their eyes. The Gobi fringes, or the whistling steppe. I remember the day I looked around the playground, saw a continent.

*

***Fornication! cried the preacher*** in a voice like a crow. He was hopping round a piece of juicy roadkill. We weren't so sure. She'd been a nice girl, one of us, before they built the road and all the trucks of history rolled through.

*

***The old man had a steam machine*** – half traction engine and half kitchen stove. He called it Moloch, half fond, half appalled by it like someone adopted for better or worse by a terrible dog. He fed it papers, page after page of his great unpublished novel, and wrote more and fed it, night by night by night. He turned grey with it, his hair was ash already, then one night his drawer was empty and he went out empty handed. After that we'd hear it roaring in the dark without him. It had started hunting for itself.

*

***The crows*** are charred remnants of a flock of birds of many colours, the only survivors of the day when fire got out of hand. The sarcasm we hear in their voices might be a warning. Not necessarily for us, still, we'd be wrong to ignore them. They are evidence. They are fingerprints that hop and fly. They could land anywhere, incriminate anyone. Including you.

*

***A crab claw*** from when this was seabed, in the middle of the island. A blown lark's egg. My disgraced and never spoken of great-uncle's wedding ring. A shell case from a skirmish in a war that reason says could not have happened. A biscuit tin of immeasurable size, tucked in a tree root, where I keep (somebody has to) the world's store of this kind of thing.

*

***Tidy your desks, said the teacher***. The headmaster, she said. An inspection. Five minutes, a chaos of tidying. Miss, miss, mine's done, please miss, look at me. Then we stood to attention. Waiting. Five minutes, ten. In the end the teacher knocked, quite shyly, on the head's door. It was open. His desk spotless, open. All his papers. Reading glasses. Cane. Outside, a large black car was just pulling away. As for the headmaster... He was never seen again.

*

***It wasn't fair*** for Katya to have two dads when some of us didn't have any. One went off to work at the sawmill, at dawn; one snuck round the back door later with a bag (never unzipped) of tools. That was one spare father, surely. So I went to school and said, in front of everyone. Later, after all the fights and shouting, people said that I couldn't have known what I was saying; she's only small, the poor innocent mite. That's how little they knew.

*

***Changeling!*** said my mother in a sudden rage. Look at your eye-brows, they meet in the middle. You weren't born with ears like that. It's the way you watch me. And the soup boils over every day. It was her face that changed, since dad – all soggy but smouldering, like a house after the firemen. I couldn't move. Stop staring, she said. Run back to the woods where you belong.

*

***She sent me to smiling lessons*** in the church hall. A Youth League leader ran them. He knows how to do it, she said, he's read all the books. I stopped in the doorway. You could come too, I said. Too late for that, said mother. You, though, there's still hope, you can do it for all of us, if you get in practice young.

*

***New times make for new entertainments*** nor does a small war put an end to it. Take the local sport of whammocking – each village sends a team of lads with cudgels, round a field of molehills. They take turns to make a dash and flatten them, one at a time. The poor moles. Except one of the heaps conceals a piece of unexploded ordnance. Everybody knows this, though of course not which. They still play.

*

***Quick, down into the cellar!*** There was a rumbling, so low that it could be in the ground or in the air. Don't move, don't speak, don't even think till I tell you they're gone. No questions. Run. We were pushed into the damp dark, all potato sacks and worse. Oy, said a voice, go easy. It was the people from the time before. And the time before that. Pray, said a faint voice from the farthest corner, have the Vikings gone?

*

***Soft tumps under the pine-litter*** – some are hut-sized enclosures, prehistoric, except that here and there torn concrete like stale bread or a snapped sinew of steel rod shows through. A few are inexplicit low domes, mushrooms coming through the subsoil, ready to swell and rupture, talcum-puff their malevolent spores to the wind.

*

***Grey flames***, you couldn't say dancing. Grey flames operating in the pit. One, that is, of the kind that can open up overnight on any street. I couldn't make out whose souls he was pitchforking down there, the dim Devil, but they seemed heavy to him. Has it come to this, he muttered. Grey flames, in triplicate. Grey flames rising ever after by the book.

*

***My father wanted to be on the side of the angels***. That was why he had to slip away. I've thought about that 'side'. I see a clear pool, little insects, water boatmen, walking under the surface, on it, upside down. And the others, the pond skaters, walking past them, almost through them, without touching, on the top. Sometimes I look straight down and see a face there, a bit like my own, staring up. Is it his?

*

***My uncle has preserved himself*** in alcohol... intact? Unchanged. It's not the same. Every brisk lad-swagger, each cock of a snook of his cap, his same old battered lad-cap. Again and again and (how could his pickled hide ever change now?) oh, again.

*

***Grandmother ruled us*** by becoming almost without mass, only tension, like a cabinet of china, tinklingly brittle, atrociously sharp when she broke. Only grandfather was immune. While the rest of us cowered he became a standing, or more often sitting, stone.

*

***If I sit still enough***, the birds hop closer. Insects blunder onto me en route to flowers on the other side. Finally, the dead unpeel the papery crust of non-existence, and step out blinking in the sun.

*

***Waiting for thunder*** lasts for days here. It's so flat – the thunder has to take a census of a million trees, to work out which is tallest. There's a process to go through. Meanwhile the windows darken, dogs cower, water seems oily, everybody's voice goes shrill. I was told off for daring thin Peeter, the gangliest one in the class, to walk across the playground. I just wanted to get it over with.

*

***Somebody's son or other*** is always being drafted, sent off to the war. Not that there are wars any longer, we're assured of that. Still, each time one of them comes home he's missing something, eye, foot, finger. That seems to be the rule. It's when someone comes back without a bruise on him, that's when you need to take care.

*

***What the cat brings in*** from the forest is the usual wounded creatures, sometimes. Sometimes something stranger, and invisible. Then the cat itself backs off and cowers, appalled by the no-thing that it's caught and maimed. Or the cat runs away. The no-thing stays. People have been known to leave their homes, or burn them to the ground, because of things like that.

*

***I went to the window***, I waited, still don't know why. But minutes later they came a thin fraying skein of them. Geese, too high to guess the species, coming north for winter, and as if they snagged a thread of me I stretched out with them, for another thousand miles, drawn impossibly thin. Could I have heard it coming, the suprasensible whistle of their wingtips, from a mile high, even through these walls, these endless corridors?

*

***There were many strange things in my grandfather's toolkit*** but no one could ever account for the trepanning saw. Then again, holes have been found in skulls from the Stone Age, round holes, neatly made and healed. People guess at some urge to transcend. I see it rather as a manhole for the gods, or at least the lower class of them, to be sent down to investigate when there's a bad smell and a blockage in the drains.

*

***My uncle Märt*** was clever, even as a boy. He made a hawk kite so realistic that the rabbits froze with terror. He could walk right up behind them, pop them in his sack. Later, he got a job in State Security. Ah, as grandma used to mutter (it was just to herself, between her and her false teeth), ah, the child is father to the man. An absent father, but a father all the same.

*

***Would you rather***, goes the playground game, walk out of the village on the straight road to the east? Or to the west? Both lead out of sight, into forest and, eventually, night. Would you rather stand in the road until you're run over by the truck going this way, or that? Our village is famous as the birthplace of philosophers. Believe me. Or would you rather not?

*

***There are walls in the air***. First they build one. Then they tell you it's not there, never was, the word 'wall' is your own invention. You might not believe them, quite, but can you walk through where it isn't? No. This was an early lesson. Nothing, you say, if not trite. It's not trite. Therefore it must be nothing. Like the wall.

*

***One day a wind from the sea*** laid flat the village, all its timbers in parallel. The people likewise. One child squeezed through the slats and escaped. Was it me, she could never stop wondering, brought the windships, that day I waved at the horizon, for no reason, from the shore? Or some centuries later, the iron-head men from the south, with swords the shape of crosses and crosses like swords.

They flattened timbers crosswise, as you might expect. The child escaped. Later, others, from the north, the east, the south again... No wonder we're a shipwreck-raft of souls. No wonder that each time she squeezes through the cracks she's thinking Was it something I said, or wished for? (Mother, grandma, uncle, tell me.) Did they always, really, come for me?

*

***Anybody might choose to be sad*** for so long, then one day they take one step further out, beyond pity or wanting it. I hadn't thought of her for years. Then I read in the paper: some nobody woman, made to wait in line for a petty permission just a year too long, suddenly ups and stabs the man behind the desk. One thrust of her knitting needle, right through the eye. Crane Beak Woman, I thought. It didn't need a photograph to tell me what that official had looked like – squat, with a face like a frog.

*

***I never believed*** the things words seem to point at could be all they are. The summer house, for instance. All well enough, but it wasn't *the house of summer*, where summer went when it couldn't be with us, as the birds well knew. Where my father, those years when he *couldn't be with us*, would be, no, *is* waiting, tapping out his pipe out or stirring the bonfire, with all the time in the world.

*

***The Devil took to drinking***, no, not firewater, not moonshine from a still in a shed in the woods. That I might have respected. This was Polish vodka, cheaper than potatoes, from the village shop. Each time I saw him he was more see-through, as if the clear stuff, more than blood, was burning in his veins. Soon even his wickedness was no more than a glassy museum-case exhibit of its former self. I wanted to smash it, he might have got free. Or he might have been all liquid and trickled away through the cracks in the floor.

*

***Grandmother came at us*** with goose fat at the first hint of a cold. She dusted out the bread crock with a goose's wing. That was quaint. And unhygienic, mother added. Me, I had a queasy feeling too. It took me years to see it: grandmother herself was the goose. Plucked painfully. The way she hissed when angry, that should have been the clue.

*

***Oh, mother***, mother, always dusting. So much of the dust must be me. Hairs, skin flakes, healed scabs, tears dried with a little crusty stain. They all went into your dustpan. Really, you must have kept more of me that way than I ever gave you of my livingbreathing self. Did you keep it, I wonder. Could we assemble a new me from the bits and start again?

*

***Radio frequencies from no-go places*** overseas. They seep in at edge of the dial, like mould marks round the window. Languages just off the coast of understanding. You think I can close my mind to them, any more than my mother could watch the fabric of the house begin to crumble, damp with lack of love?

*

***He got out of the fat black car*** with a swarm of them, four, five grandchildren who looked just like him, only tiny, bright, chippy as hornets and bristling with toys. He looked old and heavy tired, poor Devil. I softened, I admit it – went over and whispered Quick, I'll attract their attention; you make a break for it, into the thicket, now!

*

***There's a house in the woods*** that's digesting itself. Sucking in its own roof, somehow chewing the timbers, crunching, spitting out the slates. Now that's gone, it's sucking in its windows. The whole forest is drawing nearer, round it, on that indraught, and the process feeds itself. Like a fire storm after bombing, only green.

*

***A calamity of gulls*** implodes around us from the rooftops. Friends, brothers (pretty rich, this, from a piracy of cold-eyed brutes in feather uniform) *Aux armes!* Just one step off the path and they're clanging in circles like fire engines out of control. Defend your fledglings! Who can blame them – being just the claws and beak that instinct wears amongst us? Only, where were they when we needed them, time and again?

*

***Imagine, said the soldier. He was drinking***, had been drinking, had a mind or what was left of it to be drinking again. Some boys at school were older than he looked. Just imagine, he said, lookout duty, night after night after night. At first, you think you see the missiles, snouts poked over the horizon. Or you stare at the stars and out of the corner, always, of your eye one of them moves. In the end you're wishing, no, you're putting bets on just a flock of snow geese, you know, the ones that showed up on radar, damned near kicked off a world war.

*

***My uncle was a joker***. See, I found this in the forest, he said, Devil-spit! Imagine a grey candle that had dripped in all directions. A splattering in midair, spat on three dimensions. Here, catch! I dropped it, the shock of it, heavy as – he laughed, he told me it *was* – lead. He kept a jam jar of old bullets, flattened at the ends. Also an old school bunsen burner, and cold water in a pail. When we got to a quivering melt – stand back – he pitched a gobbet in. It squealed and hissed, it was trying to swarm out, every drop of devilspit the seed of smaller devils. When we all cooled off, I held it in my hands: a frozen scream.

*

***Genghis Khan*** would have been struggling, if he'd stuck with the plan, if he'd made it this far to the edge. No space for horsemen, no hills to crest and sweep down like the sea. Just forest, a stockade in three dimensions, and if not that, bog. If they'd made it here, they'd have been wading, horses sunk or butchered. They'd have been inventing oilskins, thigh-length boots, and patient attitudes. They'd have gazed at the sky, grown philosophical, rather than hungering for horizons. They'd have arrived here different, at some distance from each other, lost on their own thoughts. Something like... or maybe they were, they are, they were always, us?

*

***Yes, autumn: damp air ripening*** with smells. Old people ripening with recollections. Gradual breakdown of borders between bodies (plant or animal) and air, air and rain, rain and earth and anaerobic mould. We slip across. it isn't far to go.

*

***I've never been to New York*** but not much would astonish me. I've lain down among the reed beds looking up through the parallel parallel parallel stalks to the sky. Constant flicker and buzz and bird pulse in the upper storeys. Down here, squabbles and scuffles and clanging alarms. The waterways are chock-tight, intimate, essential to the place's life. We depend. The wind blows. Everything inclines as it inclines us. On Madison Avenue don't the skyscrapers sway-bend all together when a gust blows one way? Gusts of money, gusts of panic, gusts of fame.

*

***The isle is full of notices***, curt words explaining that the place beyond this point is not. Wires, suddenly, taut as zithers. Some hum. Or when a certain wind blows, with chimes from the dog pound, they, the wires, we, and the unseen watchers, twangle.

*

***The ancestors don't have sex***, I mean, don't have one sex or the other. You can see the process starting in the old. Grandmother's moustache, the odd wiry chin-bristle. How Grandfather curves and softens round the hips. As for the ancients, disregard the high romances, they are one thing now, and whole. It's awesome, though, the way life drives a wedge called sex between us, levering fibres apart, in tension. Creaking, almost splintering. Squealing with the urgency to spring back. Into each other again.

*

***There's an invisible mountain***, I said, in the centre of the island, and as long as they believed me, it was there. They shuffled. Prove it, said big Arvid, not quite wanting to argue outright. I climbed it, I said. From the top I saw the sea all round us. Grey ships, with noses like sharks. A fat black submarine. And the towers of the Kremlin that way, and New York the other. Burning. How could I see that, tell me, if the mountain wasn't there?

*

***The saddest person in the village*** is old Helga. Not the ordinary kind of sad. This sad has been laid down gradually like peat. The blacker the deeper it goes. At a spade's depth it is fierce, a sharp taste, almost toothsome. Deeper still, some ambiguous bones. An axe blade, with... You could take it for humour, that glint in her eye.

*

***We're a backward people***, that's what we've been told. Grandfather was one. Nothing new under the sun, he'd say, yet he would read the paper every morning. I used to think grownups listened to the news to get instructions – what they'd set out pastwards to have done. Have you ever had a dream that ends in a bang? You wake to find that a door slammed, in your real room, just that moment. While that in the dream you had been hunted and arrested, tried, led out across the execution yard, then... It took hours, towards that moment. It took years.

*

***It's a simple fact of physics***, the meniscus: how at the edge of the glass the water banks up, tense, against its limits. How it makes itself into the shallow bowl to contain itself. So no wonder that it's hard to see beyond this island. The place curves space up a little, just too high to see over. You can stand on the edge and gaze out, where you think is out, and see nothing at all.

*

***The roads go off into the forest***, to what end is anyone's guess. Maybe to draw trucks out of several distances, through a haze of diesel, gradually materialising into dust and rust. And music. One truck driver, from Smolensk, has heaved off on the mud verge, and is drinking. *Ya vas lyublyu*, he roars in an operatic bass. *I love you*, turning to the whole spruce chorus for support. It stays shtum. Then, *All this way*. he's sobbing. *Has it come this?*

*

***The Devil has a boss***, as his boss has, and his. So on, maybe forever. You can see the weight of that shuddering pile, it's what gives the Devil his stoop. It's not, he says, that he's lost faith in what he's doing, just... there's less devilry in it. I used to go through the world, he says, like a fox with its tail on fire. And sighs.

*

***The little boy scribbled*** out his parents' faces in his schoolbook. That had the teachers nodding and exchanging glances. This was thirty years back. Today he's in an office on a floor to which the public lifts don't go. Your forms spread in front of him. His ink pad, his Yes or (indelibly) No. Still, there's a whisper in the voice when people speak his name.

*

***The first graffiti*** on the island were from the age of the ice nomads. No casual spray-job, this, but granite chipped at, grain by grain. Reindeer, hieroglyphic deities in equal measure. And twig people, mere buds for a head, as if the sense of being in there had not blossomed. Men, with four stick limbs, and a fifth, a thorn, a splinter-prick. We build a first cast concrete bridge and, guess what, there they were again.

*

***Today is education***. Our good lecturer is one, in theory, with the heroes and what we don't call the saints. The great granite bookmen come down from their plinths to speak to us. With the martyrs, in theory. He's worried and grey as he speaks – to us, through us – speaks to just behind, where all our parents have been sat in rows. Some shuffling, some like children who don't dare to put their hands up, Please Sir, squirming. Many of them, oh don't think we haven't noticed, much too still.

*

***You can put up a fence in the forest*** – angle-steel posts, barbed wickedly. That sorts out the quick from the dead – the ones who only stand and gaze, the ones who walk straight through. Just ask yourself before you do it: will you sleep easier, once you know who is who?

*

***Today: the kind of day you keep the window shut*** in case you let more darkness in.

*

***I never knew anyone could be as cruel*** as Riiki. The kind of boy who knew that pulling one wing off a fly was finer sport than two. And his feel for the opening, how not-so-ruthless wannaboys could come to need, to crave, to be at his side. The way he'd lead them, old friends, on to the moment where they found the victim he had led them to, and cornered, was themselves. I felt a quickening. Girls who said I fancied him were wrong. They weren't in the same world, the new cool dimensions he was tracing round the playground, in which he was really alone but I knew that one day he was bound to turn and see me, and only me, there.

*

***A travelling cinema show*** rolled in. We had nowhere for the screen, so they set up, diesel generator throbbing, at the forest edge. The newsreel played onto the treetrunks, when you were straight on, perfectly. The rest of us caught slants and angles. Me, I crept among the shadows. There I saw a different film completely, all the figments no full-frontal film could reveal, between the spruces, running, ducking, hiding. Just like me.

*

***Redcurrant bushes*** that my father planted, and ran wild... Crawl in under, you'd be face to face with those driblets of ripening light. Red, red on the pink side of scarlet, a bodiless red, like a glint from a crack in the mirror, that escapes you when you look again. Like the taste of redcurrants: somewhere between that tart dry moistness and the bitter grit must be the sweetness. Somewhere. One at a time, I rolled them round my tongue, the tip, side, tip, but never found it, quite.

*

***Nobody will love you***, Mother said suddenly, if you look at them like that. Even the cat, see, bristles. Don't say 'Look at them like what?' Like you're looking at me now. She was slicing an onion. Two flavours of tears. We could get you some glasses, she said, thick ones, you might pass as short-sighted. Oh, child. Tell me, if you're so sharp, then, what will become of us?

*

***The first car on the island*** has only grown grander. Too grand now to go by the road, now that's given up to trucks and motorbikes. It withdrew to old man Kirik's back yard, then in a high sulk to his threadbare barn. It filled out with the rust, in the dark, like a man of substance wears a little weight. Last time I crept in there I had to curtsey – backed out, shuffling. It will be there when the barn and all the rest of us have crumbled. Like a longship in a grave mound. First and last.

*

***At the end of his life, grandfather's vegetables*** were singular. They were one of each kind. One cauliflower he halved each mealtime, to infinity. One carrot as thick as tree trunk, a thinner slice each time enough to make a stew. It's not that he couldn't afford more, but then, he too was singular. Old Noah, lading one of each kind, travelling light now, and who dared ask him what was the point of a one-by-one ark?

*

***We are already in the afterlife***, where I can sit down with my wicked greatgranduncle Nurme, at a pavement cafe table in the dark heart of the wood. He leans towards me – Show 'em, girl, don't waste a stick of your tinder that could start a fire – with his three-toothed grin. don't waste a splinter that could smart under somebody's skin. There's father, dandling his not-yet born great-grandchild. At first he doesn't turn when I come up behind them. He turns. He's saying something, but I'm too distracted by the surface of this world, the noise of present living. He's speaking. I can't understand him yet.

*

***The real ghosts*** in this place aren't the dead. The dead are vivid — flash-glints off dark water, in whatever tarmac puddle, culvert, drainage ditch. The ghosts are the ones who've given up on living, with their lost loves/lands/hopes, mousey-shredded self-respect. It's a kind of listless treason. I know they can't resist. But still, they're punished. Life. Internal exile. They go on and on.

*

***When people leave, they leave*** an absence, just the size and shape they were. A parting gift. Later, some of the absences lie down like old people and fade, decently. Some, like raw abandoned children, grow, and change, and grow.

*

***I've had enough, said mother***. These cracked hands, this skin raw as if the chicken had plucked me, as if the sink had scoured me. Ashes inside as if the fire had rattled the grate of me, banked high, consumed me. Lines round my eyes, from peering into distances or corners, looking where everyone's gone. They're yours now, your inheritance, believe me. The mirror might lie to you for a few more years, but you'll see. And don't think you can blame me then, she said. I'll be gone.

*

***The weasel*** goes through the grass like a skilled insinuation. What's to hold her? She has young, which she loves, in the burrow, waiting in a bristling fizzing knot. She has to kill.

*

***An underglade*** of makeshift crosses in the forest, just a few steps off the road. Twigs, accidental windwrack almost, except they're tied with plaited grass. And the cause or story? Buried with whatever's buried. Still, there'll be more, count them, any time you stop to see.

*

***One of my teachers was full of questions***, so much that I thought he must be empty inside; all our answers didn't seem to be enough to fill him up. He asked us about sums, geography and verbs and, bit by bit, our relatives too. Sometimes he wrote things down, as if they were too heavy for one head to hold. So I learned about questions. How sometimes there'd be strangers on the doorstep, who seemed to know exactly what you'd said.

*

***I've never been afraid of the dark***. Why would you? You would have to be afraid of all those inside spaces in your body. (Some are.) You'd have terrors several times a minute when you blink. And as for your blood, which works in the dark, in its tunnels, mute as miners... It's a riot, it's a red flag, when it sees the light of day.

*

***Grandmother snores***. It doesn't sound easy, how she sleeps. It's the grappling of cogs, unoiled, joints grinding, flutterings of flywheels. It's the windmill in the forest. Grist and gristle. Bones and bellows. It's the machine that loves us, in the end.

*

***I got everything right*** in the test and got smacked for it, I must have cheated. Confess, said teacher, and I couldn't, so that made it worse. Next time I cribbed the right mistakes from Nina, who was dim and popular. I got one wrong – that is, right. Nina smacked me later, because teacher thought she must have cribbed from me, and smacked her first.

*

***We're never short of puzzles***. Like that fallen bough, charred at the point it fractured. Who kindled a fire in the crook of it, ten feet up the tree? I know I talked about the fire owl, but that's just a story. On the other hand, a story can combust, spontaneously.

*

***When I grow up, I used to think, I want to live so slow*** that even amber is a liquid, a drop that melts in my palm. Glass is a fine fall like water, that distorts the world a little as it goes. Coal is the sun's heat first collapsing into matter, then splitting free again. When I grow up, yes. I might have to wait.

*

***On a midsummer night the sky*** is whitish green, the colour of water melting out of snow. All this, I think, could be a bubble, like a swimming spider drags down and anchors in among the pebbles of the stream. Imagine, that silvered globe, small world of air, and you inside it. Silence, on the strike of midnight. All the world of water frothing, rushing, overhead.

*

***The old couple next door*** learned to dance the tango one day, suddenly. No one knew how, but there were rumours. Someone tipped off the authorities. When the knock at midnight came they caught them at it. But no gramophone. No radio tuned to foreign stations, no suspect literature. The policeman said (how did he know?) they danced it perfectly. The old man said it just came to them one night, because they loved each other, tragically. That, and looking at the moon.

*

***Grandfather didn't die*** but simply, bit by bit, dispersed. His hearing, first. It went into the squeal-and-chitter of the small birds, at the edge of anybody's senses. Then into the middle ranges, seagulls, crows. His eyesight left him, grew quivering whiskers, scuttled off into the underbrush. His strength went into the wind, his movement into simmerings of swallows in the eaves. Their restless readying, then, one day, gone.

*

***Red chickens***, out of their chickenwire cantonment, pucking, clecking, comfortably gormless, on the loose. If I was them I'd make a dash for it, knowing what I know. Then again, just how happy does that make me, to the nearest peck of grain?

*

***The spiders are coming indoors*** for the autumn. Cousin Janno whimpers. This has taught me plenty. Like... the more scared you are, the more they'll find you. The faster they'll scuttle. They jiggle and twitch on the tingling wires in your head. No, no, I try to tell him, each one picks up a grain of your panic and makes off with it, back under the floorboards. For her young. Is that meant to make me feel better, says Janno. Now he's scared of floorboards too. He moves over them fast, like a spider, on the tips of his toes.

*

***The truck veered*** off the straight road through the forest. It was three a.m. It came straight at me, said the driver. It was no shape, wings flared, like smoke with eyes and beak. Smells of diesel and braised rubber and ripped spruce. He crawled out of the wreck. They say he was lucky. Or unlucky. I'd say he'd been blessed.

*

***Sometimes, smoke*** seems to be trying to write its own name. Cursively, but failing. Or to read the message that it carries, curling round and back to grasp, to try to grasp, itself, to give a name to what it is.

*

***There was an empty farm***. I knew the way, though the paths, and the clearing itself, were closing. No one would live there. We knew bad luck clung. Whispers said the people there had gone into the forest, one day, with a shotgun, just like that. I dreamed of a tree, an old pine, creaking, with a shotgun in its crook. Older (but not much) I went to look. The woodpile was putting out green pine needles. Knot holes in the timbers made witch's-moles of twigs. In all the cracks, smug moss. A window cracked, a tightening of spider webs, that was enough. The house was following its owners. Not long now, it would be forest. And we'd follow, each, every one of us, all go to the forest one by one.

*

***I've tried my best to be*** my mother. Here's her duster, here's her five in the morning, her internal exile, here's her sigh. I've tried to be my father. His wherever. Grandmother, grandfather, I could go on. My unborn siblings, too, and half the village. What drove them away? All this points to an answer. I'd rather not say.

*

***A little wire-haired girl*** comes down the pavement, seriously. She's not not-looking, but her gaze is like a waitress balancing a high-stacked and chinkling tray. On it, her whole life. Awed by the importance, I step into the road to let her by, the way one would a whole convoy: jeeps, trucks and a low-loader with a canvas-wrapped and unnameable load. Which as it happens is what bears down the road towards me. Now I have to choose.

*

***Rain comes over the world*** dense as another forest, grey and at a wind-slant. I don't want to be out of it. Here, the air is stopped, like a fist in its own mouth. It could stifle, and me with it, except on the grey skylight's underside something has been gathering. Now it hits me, one drip, in the forehead and I shatter. White light, all my fizzing watts exploding, the world rushing in. Like grace, a veil of momentary splinters.

*

***In some places the air*** has a bruised feel, who knows how long since whatever happened. Touch it, the place recoils. The space is taut with gazes stretched into, beyond, the distance. Some straining out behind the mute trucks leaving; others, being taken, reaching back.

*

***I've seen a man beaten*** until he was sick. Blood in it. And the men who did it, turning to me: Now see what you, you and your kind, made us do.

*

***I held down a job for a while*** in the sawmill, doing the accounts. Countless logs, times ten for planks, a hundred for fence posts, twenty thousand for the matchsticks with which my uncle made his model of the Kremlin. One night he struck one, accidentally. We all went up in flames.

*

***I've got all day, said the policeman***. I can wait. I've got the rest of my life, I said. That, he said, is what you think. Now he was smiling. Oh, I've got it, I smiled back, whatever the hell you do. Someone looking through the window, they'd have thought that we were lovers. Interrogation as a form of flirting. Maybe in another world it is, we were.

*

***The questions*** when they come are cold and as precise and self-delighting as a snipers' party in the woods. All the people I've been either scatter or fall. Only the eight-year-old, quick stick-legs, has the skinny wit to stand dead straight, dead still, behind a tree.

*

***They held me down*** and I struggled. Shrank, lashed, writhed right out of my skin. Was a cat-spit, a weasel, a slippery tangle. A trouble with teeth. I was in all directions, was water, I poured through their grip. I overflowed the moment, and the century, I was in, I was the forest, voices in the wind. Was all the ever calling, crying and confessing, it was all me. I would come back for this girl, this name, this body later. Ergo sum.

*

***And suddenly, a stillness***. As if everything faced inwards, that moment, with a kind astonishment. Or everything faced outwards and felt very small. As if no mistake could be unmade or made, or had been ever. As if you hadn't been there, as if this needed to be said. As if you didn't know.

*

***I am willing to answer*** your questions if you let me choose my language. Today it has to be that of the swans, the great whoopers. They should know a thing or two we don't. But you must let me see the sky, because distance is part of their syntax. Their speech makes no sense without it, not to them or to us.

*

***I think I might have misled you***, making you think I had a secret to confess. Or I wanted to have one, just to feel the difference between us – surface tension, one side knowing, one side not, and in between the tingling, a shared skin, neither yours nor mine. Even the way you press against it, hurting. If I knew, I'd say. If I knew there were words for what I know, I'd say Wait. Since I know there aren't words for it, all I can do for us is say Read this.

*

***I read a Western*** once. The plot escapes me. All I remembered was smoke signals. After that the cowboys could go on without me, and the railroad and the rest. I was with the Injun, just one, on the horizon, who had to gather the brushwood, and the tinder, and the moist leaves, to tease out one long clear huff, then two. Slowly, half a mile high, above the endless prairie. Before its endlessness came to an end. I wanted to do that. So I do now, in a space as small as this.

*

***The forest has no secrets***. Every detail declares itself – *me, here!* – in its way. But so many, you gather them up by the armful, you drop them, you leave empty-handed. If I had a secret, I would take it to the forest. It would be safe there. I would sing it out loud, like a bird.

*

***Whether this is forest***, *a* forest, or *the* forest, we don't have to say. Ours is a language without articles, and without their absence, too. Can you imagine that, to be held to no distinction? One day I live in one forest, next day in another. Bring your phrase book and your primer, catch me if you can.

*

***Speak to me, softly***, in your different language, its slippery consonants. The closer I lean in to hear, or speak back, the more our breaths whiten the pane between us. Tiny temperature gradients, and where they meet, inevitably, condensation. It will end in tears.

*

***You've got to meet me***, you say, in the language that prevails. The public space. The common place. Where else, you say, can we be? I say, The forest. And yes, you know what I mean.

*

***It's not what you said*** just now that matters. I scarcely remember. It's the shape, the heft, of silence afterwards. You'll say it's much the same with me. What a delicate labour, then: to craft this bone-china vessel between us, with our four clumsy hands. To carry the weight of what's not in it, that's almost too heavy to bear.

*

***The force that keeps us*** circling round each other is, you must agree, our contradiction. If I loved you, I would let you hold me. If you loved me, you would set me free.

*

***Have you ever been outside*** that cool gaze you turn on the world, looking back in? It's another kind of cold out here, I'm shivering, can't you see?

*

***I'm arranging my life for you***, in order, A to Z. My confessions, in index card size. I would do them in barcode format if I could – let no one tell you that I don't cooperate. And now you face me with your different alphabet. You must have noticed, we have sounds that don't translate. Certain silences too.

*

***It goes without saying...*** That's your gambit. Mine: Without saying, it goes. After that is silence. Both watching. Everything hangs on who makes whom move next.

*

***You roll them yourself***, each as thin as a twig. Collapse it quickly into smoke, and roll again. You could well afford to buy or to fix yourself Balkan Sobranie, this is affectation, this is how you show the world how serious you are. Now you breathe out, and the air is full of visible disintegration, I am in it with you, you have that much power, at least. Whether to meet your eye or not, that is my freedom. Your blue eye, I decide today. See? I can choose.

*

***Silence. You did that to me once***. That kind of silence. Now you round on me, Tell us, tell us everything... Dumb insolence, you say, you call my silence now, and raise your fist. Go on, slap, hit, you'll break your knuckles on it. One day, beyond all this, I'll come into another kind of silence. I will simply hold my peace.

*

***I caught us, you, me, in the garden*** – our reflection, that is, in the window as the daylight went. Those two, free to get up and go and yet, they were leaning that close, eyes wire-strung to each other's, tense-tingling, as if tightening something, dare by dare, right to the brink. Like a love or a deal.

*

***Today, I acknowledge the door.*** That's progress, you say. You stub out a butt, lean back. Wait. Tomorrow I may acknowledge the lock. The keyhole. Your eye in it, watching. I do not concede this is reality.

*

***The hurt gull*** tumbles down the chimney. Hunkers in the dark back corner, with its barb-tipped beak. All the child wants is to mend it. Feed it fish scraps, keep it for its own good. Make it see sense about life as a pet. The child almost loves the scars the beak leaves, every time the child reaches in. You think it's another of my *once-upon-a*'s, don't you? What have I got to write with in here but my beak's nib, a drop of your blood.

*

***What will you trade me*** for the part of me you've taken? You don't see the need to bargain, it's a done deal, is that what you think? What you've got comes from my past, sure as if you'd sat down with my parents when I was a thing of six. What I'll have comes from your future, and you won't know when or how. Look into my eyes, I can see you believe me. So where are we now?

*

***You weren't listening***. Very well then... I finessed the packet of Rizlas you fiddle with, trying to think. There you go patting your pockets, brushed by the ghost of your need. And me? Crisp see-through pages, space enough to write you this. Our smoke notebook. Now I'll watch you draw my words down deep inside you, without knowing. Hold them, frown a moment. Nod. Exhale. Crave more.

*

***A fine rain*** smoking downwards, round the single streetlamp. Or is the spilled light steaming upwards? Two illusions passing through each other, each so sure of its own story. Like me through you, like you through me.

*

***I'd I didn't exist***, some far-flung theory tells me, someone else would just have to be me. The time and place requires us, and the language that's the flux in which we swim. If you weren't sitting there opposite, now, then chance would throw random atoms into that conjuncture, that force field quivering, and they'd hang there, looking at me with the same strained kindness, saying Own up, are these your words, this your name at the bottom, this the moment when you'll stop shapeshifting and confess?

*

***She came to the end of the sentence*** like, well, a woman coming to the end of a sentence. Stalled at the gates of the prison, almost empty suitcase in her hand. Looking round, with just a bus fare, as free as a cage bird busted out. Appalled. She took a breath. Recidivist. *As I was saying…* she began.

*

***She had already left home***, up to a point. She had left home at home, where it had been, sure that she'd find it there when she returned. Wrong. They'd sent it after her, without a forwarding address.

*

***She lost heart***. After that she travelled lighter. Words resonated deeper in the cavity. Sometimes she wished she could climb into that space, curl up. Hide from the heart which might trail home one day, like a stray cat, yowling at her door.

*

***She went to the city and came back*** some years later both bigger and smaller than when she left. Stretched and diminished. As if she'd taken the A to Z, and the phone book and the fictional timetables on the bus stop, and all the faces in the queue, taken all that inside her. You could see the circulation of it, both sluggish and urgent, in her veins – see it right through her skin, which almost transparent, like a bag of shopping she's struggling home to lay out on the kitchen table, for all the people who're no longer there.

*

***She looked for her roots*** on the island. Hopelessly. No wonder: no plant looks for its roots. Its roots are its kind of looking. Sharper than ours, with hair-fine tips, how it sees in the dark, the damp, the mould. To say 'look for one's roots' is to be already not the tree, but a twig, a bird on the twig, a note on its tiny gristle ocarina, a breath in a space in a throat of a bird.

*

***She...*** She... Hold on. Who? Who said 'she'? She was only what I told you. Who says 'I', for that matter? Or 'said'? Sometimes we stand on the edge (together) of a great abyss.

*

***The university of things...*** Winter stars, between branches: architecture of what's not so much known as laid open to a knowing, like God's eye, if He had an eye, if there was God. The towers and halls and convocations are all round us, nakedly. We are and aren't admitted – tradespeople, cleaners even, scuttling through the high lanes, in the still-dark, before the gifted students, the birds, wake and preen and begin.

*

***That's not smoke*** in the creases of forest. Nor is it people in hiding there, living or dead. It's not even our hope or our fear that they might be there somewhere, but the having heard once, in a voice as smudgy-dull as graphite: You needn't think that the forest will hide you, nor silence, nor equivocation. If you are against us, we will smoke you out.

*

***I become invisible*** quite easily. The stealth of a birch on the forest edge, not looking for darkness but standing aside, letting everybody's gaze go by. Or uncrumpling myself just enough, like a fertiliser bag, stop-and-start down the pavement as if with slight intentions of its own. It's not hard. It's the reappearing that's a challenge, now and then.

*

***It can always get colder***. If you hear yourself saying 'cold', with never mind how many fuckbugger words, then rest assured, it will. If you can say or think at all. We had a man, mother Keskus's son, came back from twenty years in a place with no name. But north, north. He no longer spoke, he never uttered, as if his tongue stayed frozen to his palate, words lodged in his larynx, ice-crystallised – only to be coughed up, streaked with blood, the night he died.

*

***The spiders*** are working in the tree roots, as they have forever. Misty funnel-webs, small whorls of implication. We built houses; they were there in the eaves. We started to think. What might it all mean. Now most of us have spiders spinning in our brains. These days I look up and there are white threads, sticky, to and fro across the wide blue sky.

*

***And overnight, snow***. A new order of things. Its first act is a dizzy abolition of the law of gravity. Implausible spires of it balance on twigs, weightless. That's before the grey and dumbstruck mass of it bears down, out of the wastes. First our cars and footsteps slow, then months, weeks, days, till there's no counting.

*

***The birches*** are trees of unsettlement. Where the forest is advancing, where it's been hacked back. Uncertain clearings. There's a dust of orange lichen this year on the windward sides. Odd, then, that we see them and think: *home*. Or perhaps not: birch, its awkward poise, its twisting lightwards. Its unmendably scarred grace.

*

***A swathe of scrub*** through virgin pinewood: sparse heath, gorse, low-creeping bloody cranesbill, small tormentil like the flames of gas turned down to a sputter. Mountain land, but flat. So flat you look this way and that – a straight alignment. If you kick at the grit, an inch or two and then hard standing, tarmac crumbles up like stale cake for the birds. An airstrip. At the far end, the stump of a tower. Like a moth's, the radar antenna would sweep and sweep the darkness blindly, with blind fear and appetite.

*

***It comes over me sometimes*** – a great stillness in which, at the same time, every still thing stirs. The table, the lampstand, wooden things recall their lives as trees. Stone walls hark back to bedrock. Even the concrete crumbles into its creation: water, engine grease, the vodka sweat of the bloke who backed the truck up and kicked the shute open. Its sludgy rumble, and his curses too.

*

***The marsh pool on a frosty morning:*** threads of vapour from the milky surface. A continual giving up of ghosts.

*

***I saw myself going by*** outside the window. I wanted to run out and follow her. It's a temptation. The forest's there, still some corners haven't been discovered. Feral children crouching, over bone and berry banquets, in the undergrowth. And I saw myself inside, looking out. I didn't recognise the house, or the man at her side. His uniform, still crisp from her pressing. The way his lips curled up beneath his fine moustache at the smell of her cooking, the slight tang of berry and bone. But no, let them go.

*

***Winter, and the sea ice*** moves around the island, imperceptibly. Nudges its muzzles against it, creaking, wheezing, lowing slightly like pale cattle. You think that sounds cute? Have you ever been surrounded in a gateway by a lumber-throng of restless moos, all crazed by vague affection – hooves, teats, scabs, blowflies, splatter-dung enough to swamp the planet, not to mention you?

*

***So many birds come northbound***, in their season. In their season, south again. We live in their slipstream. Always our gaze drawn, our breath sucked after them. And yet, given chance to go, or no choice, then we yearn to stay.

*

***Salt decides***, out on the headland. What lasts: fish salted and hung up to dry, low flesh-leathery plants, spine-bushes. Steel on the other hand rusts and weeps away. Beyond that, stones, in their thin salted glitter. Then only the sweep of early warning radar. Wind. The froth of a dim shoal, miles out. A thin smoke of gulls, rising around a notion that's possessed them. Diving and rising, rising.

*

***Why do I wake up*** with vertigo some mornings? I clutch at the sides of the bed. But this is a place without edges – flat, trees snug up to the house and no horizon. A metre or three above sea level, no tides, what's to worry? Listen. Silence. Not a murmur of a foreshock. And yet, we could fall and fall and fall.

*

***Progress is a cargo cult***, on this island where nothing much moves. It comes gleamy, slightly battered, from the container washed up by the storm. We can see it's machinery, white goods. The packet shows a happy family, but where to plug them in? The manual seems to talk of something quite else. A kind of power tool. Should it ever get started, I can see that it has teeth.

*

**Time was** that cargoes were the dream. Children would sit on the shore, like me, and be transported. Now container ships pass behind the farther islands, higher than them, you can see the blockhouse of the cabin moving all the way along. Now it's the island, it's us, who are dreamlike. A dream of somewhere where a flagless crew-man – how many on that great hulk. maybe ten at most – might wave to a child like his daughter, or me, waving. Where he dreams he might belong.

*

***Everything will be all right***, we're told now. Sense will be made of everything. We live in an expanding universe, at the limit of which, like a silvery wall, is happiness, with our huge faces in it. Quite beyond our wit to see beyond.

*

***No one hunts any more***, the convenience store is so much closer. Which means there isn't much for him to do, the mad gamekeeper. He still fancies he's beating the bounds for the old baron who employed him, or his grandfather, the odd hundred years ago. Nobody poaches. So he takes time to line them up, the approachable animals, and gives them lectures on the joy of being eaten by humans of the more discerning sort.

*

***I watched the piledriver*** chugthump all day They were trying to peg the edge of the land into place, with a jetty, or maybe to staple the sea. Down, down, the pile went. Went on going. Steel rods, concrete, girders, nothing stayed. It was early evening when the foreman cracked and wept. I could have told them. Nothing in this land resists you. Everything a land can say says Stranger, come on in.

*

***Some nights the smell of forest rises***, pine litter and mould, up through the concrete or linoleum. Put me on Persian carpet, it would be the same. Then I have to lie down, curl up like a bear in the tree roots or a partisan with just the single bullet in his gun. Wake us at your peril, from our old dreams, in our rank-as-mushrooms, raggy-pelted body heat.

*

***We had a mad Dane*** striding round the gun emplacements trying to get haunted by his father's ghost. Or maybe to become his own. We get a lot of that these days. They come with celebrity yachts and motor cruisers, little windbreaks on the beach. They leave tanned to a shadow, and allergic to the light of day.

*

***Our sea is almost captive***, a lake with a leak, with tiny short-breathed tides and barely brine enough to salt a herring. Still, or maybe for this reason, it can turn, storms rise from nowhere, re-define a ship of living souls as memories. And next morning wear a pale innocent light like the first day again.

*

***The grand house worries too much*** about foundations. All that effort to lift itself out of the damp, the murmurs of bog, its bad shiftless accents. Build in wood, we could have told them, we know stone will sink and damp will rise. The old manor house was a fine speech in a foreign language, on tiptoe looking twenty miles over our heads towards its neighbour, and where is it now? We watch newcomers pouring concrete, laying a damp course, and think Shall we tell them? No. In time, in time.

*

***Something's hissing*** out there in the darkness. Listen, when the wind drops, it's hardly a sound, the way a silence seethes. The old people had names for them, first not spoken, then forgotten. For what whispers. What might not have faces, but takes shape now and then. As sparks. A farmhouse burns down. It's the nearest we can come to a translation, the rush of the flame.

*

***The career of a tree*** is not what people think. Not that year-on-year of escalating self-exposure to the sky. It's the way it folds itself, in on its heartwood, ring by ring of silence. So it grows.

*

***The place the streams flow to*** and go to ground there, that's the pilgrimage, a kind of pole. Any old culture can worship the source. On grey days, when by chance you find it, you'll see two or three old people nearby, where you can't be certain where an edge begins, is that you or the ground unsteadied. You'll find wish-scraps, love-knots, curses, offerings snagged in the grass, where the water's brought them this far then, it's not its business, left them with us and gone on alone.

*

***More land is rising toward us*** inch by inch out of the sea. I think of the drowned. How much more reticent will they have to become, to keep their privacy?

*

***An itinerant hulk*** of granite, at the tideline. Knee deep. The stunned fixity of its where-am-I-now, the millennial morning-after of the Ice Age. An erratic, they say, as if this was just a mistake. (Give or take a few years, we're all terminal moraine.) Pathetic, no? Consider the glacial grouting out, grubbing up, mountains, valleys levelled, in the scouring of their broken selves upon their selves. That smooth-cheeked cheek, it's not innocence, it's abrasion. All it has helped to destroy.

*

***Between our land and sea, always***, the reed beds. Is that why the tide scarcely moves – the million stalks pin it in place? If they gave, or if the fabric ripped, it might pour away, outwards, to the smooth lip of the world's-edge waterfall. Where would we be then? Swept, with it, over. Or on a bare shore, shivering in the wind across the rocky plain.

*

***My cousin has migraines*** and keeps thinking I can see them, pointing at the neon jizzles they make in the air. I try to say it's no good, there's a whole dimension missing – they're at no distance, from him or from me. It's when he looks into my face, looks closely: there, he says, tracing their ripples down my cheek. I feel myself dissolving, back into atoms, their shivering pulses that make something of the void in which we live.

*

***This time they were playing*** intently out behind the water butt. Whatever they'd been saying, they just watched as I went by. I've seen them deeper in the woods, not wise, but who am I to warn them? I thought I could escape my children simply by not having them. How naive can you be?

*

***All sorts of music wash up*** at the tideline. Shanties and lieder are the least of it. Today, a shard of heavy metal from a passing German tanker. It groaned on the shingle, going tinny, adenoidal. Catching distance like a head cold. Anger, fretted to a plaintive yapping: hell-hounds on the far shore of the black lake, puppies really, set off by the beat of swans into the darkness, and their master never comes.

*

***Shake the tree,*** pine needles sprinkle on the paper. Each over any, at angles, here, in rows. Later the fire ants come, a plague of commas. So we scatter, so we too are read.

*

***A thin curving sandspit*** runs into the bay. Beyond reason. How far can you walk with sea all round you? Only, on the one side, it bristles and rucks. On the other, harbours pure reflection. And still further: barely a stagger's-breadth wide, then water glints between the pebbles. Still a dotted-line of taller stones breaks surface, that much further. Beyond that is wading and faith. As long as there's the difference, calm one side, insurgent on the other, you could walk all day. And further. Westward, where the sunset waits.

*

***We are always*** on the cusp, we live there. Don't let our settled habitations fool you, our flat land, how we dwell on the past. Any old moment, the horizon's rolling at us, a gathering wave. Through chance, through the cells of our bodies, through the ways our bodies touch. It heaves, a water-hill that's its own watershed, the cresting ruck of What-next…at the same time as Already is collapsing into what we are, in scars, in screes, of striped foam, hissing backwash other languages might call the future-present tense.

*

***Dusk, and lights*** come on inside the narrow windows of… It might be your old school, a railway station, a cheap drinking joint or a monastic hostelry. It doesn't matter, it doesn't exist, it's just me saying. The point is, did you see yourself inside, watching the windows darken? Pulling the curtain. Or here, at the forest edge, sky still green-glass, houses like a fragile tea set on a table laid for God knows who.

*

***Next door the baby*** starts to wake. At first it's a creaking, then a sound like struggling with a cussed, shapeless weight. Now that thin wedge of sound is levering her heavy parents out of bed, into motion. All over the world, in the dark, babies are waking, squirming, bracing their mighty little selves against the boulder-ness of being. Heave. So the planet rolls on.

*

***We're going now***, they said, the young dead who used to meet me in the forest. Going, but not going anywhere. When I looked again they were mist, or less, a pearly lustre in the air. Drops quivering on twig tips. Silence (which maybe always was what they were saying) newly resonant…

*

***It doesn't matter***, you could cut down the forest, you could drain the bogs and grub up the creatures from their stinky burrows. I've been to the city, I've seen them – claw scrapes on the tarmac. Sudden sump holes in the rush hour street. The clabber of bone beaks, cries like brake squeal panic. People learn to think it's only traffic, the sound the earth exhales when the traffic lights change, but they're wrong.

*

***No one calls***. I haven't spoken for so long that my language sits by the window, doing crosswords. Five o'clock – my appetite is in the kitchen, searching the pantry, beginning to prowl. My feet quite want to join it, my head's OK in the easy chair. My tongue and my breath are toying with a dum-de-something, possibly a hymn tune. I could start to feel outnumbered. Someone, come and call!

*

***The news about mountains was bad***. The highest in the world had been climbed, when I was one year old. Quite what a mountain was, I still couldn't have said — I mean, look at this island. A few last fierce ones were still being picked off. I imagined the last, behind bars or in some reservation. Too tragic. I wanted it to break out. Head west. Come and hide, however hopelessly, here.

*

***If something was buried here***, in the clearing, we would know. Or rather, not us, but the frost, the way it contours shadows. The slight different lushnesses of sorrel, maybe evidenced, to discerning palates, in the sharpness of its taste. The soil itself is saying something, or is holding its breath, years, a century on, the way a child who witnessed something might live in the shock like a brittle cocoon.

*

***The last time I saw the Devil*** he was quite deflated. Slumped on a bench. All his randy and ravenous belching bragging grandeur long gone. He looked like a ruptured puffball. Puffed out. All those tiny spores of wicked scattered on the wind. Feel them, grit in your eye, or itching where you can't reach. Peppering the papers, statutes, rulebooks – they might look like stops and commas but they are the snags, every bureaucrat knows, on which the future, yours and mine included, hangs. Even now.

*

***All this seems a long time ago*** although it isn't. Or is and always was already. Is that's what it's like for the old, time breaking up like ice in the spring thaw? Stay back from the edge, said mother, from the bank, from where the falls were just unlocking. But who wouldn't want to inch a little nearer, is that what grandma was doing, without moving? Just to look.

*

***The ones who have gone***, first there's a silence in their places, then it closes over, until soon you don't even see the blind spots in your sight. Only, you can feel something has leached out of things, of people even, that remain. When I was a child I'd suck a slice of watermelon gently, for the longest time, till only the crisp pale dry shape of its flesh was left in my hands. And suddenly feel sorry, for or to it, in the way that history does not.

*

***A cormorant***, straight and fast, across the bay to nowhere. So low that the downbeat of its wings fits the wave trough, and the next peak lifts it. Or (ask my mad grandfather, he sees everything contrary) the bird shapes the sea for us daily. When the last one dies, the sea will never move again.

# TRANSLATING SILENCE

## Now, in Vaikus

History: landscape. Landscape: history.
A landscape with no mountains, with no border.
Land made for marching over
by whichever empire now may be in ebb or flow.

A landscape hard to defend,
not hard to vanish into,
so when the new masters look,
there you are, gone.

*

Wind in the reedbeds. More than head high, rushes swaying
as the wind leans on them, one way, then the other.

I've come looking for the edge, the tangled coast I saw
from a mile high, up among the airwaves –

Finnish, Russian, Swedish, German, several slants of English
and Estonian – airwaves tangling till they are the calling

of migrating birds. From up there it looked clear.
Down here, it's close, but never there to touch.

Wind in the reedbeds. For a moment a wind path opens,
like the Red Sea, as if something passed through,

close. Something web-foot, not minding that the ground
has gone beneath it, water glittering between the stems.

Turn back. At the end of the track, a wooden house;
from somewhere, family voices. And a child, it must be,

practising a trumpet, none too well. When I get there
the house is empty as if it's been empty for years.

*

One duck... One other
further off. (They are not multiple)

One flip-splash, out
of being. For a long time, nothing.

Where it bobs up, you already know,
will not be where you thought to look.

Two swans, equally. Now and then a gull.
Each a separate incident, not
'unrelated' but related on a scale I don't expect to see.

One crow's croak. Across the water, one house, and another,
in the far woods; there are villages, I know, and have to believe,

but this evening's lesson is on the one-ness of things.
Their one-by-one-ness, all together. This is more than unity.

*

Even in a tiny country
there's a kind of forest that goes on for ever.

You drive for an hour
on a straight road, straight and flat.
You never reach a rise to see beyond.

Instead, right and left, bare trunks
of spruces, like fencing. Then
like a crack in the surface of seeing,
one chance glimpse could open

and close – too shutter-quick to un-see,
even if you wanted, and it's let you in.

*

A slight turn in the path, a light-
filled clearing. A moment. A stillness
that's sudden, surprising, a gasp, a thrill –
all the things stillness is not supposed to be.

Deep, yes. Not dark. Powder-green reindeer moss
glows upwards from the scrimmage where a tree has been,
has fallen, deadwood mined to a cinnamon dust
by ants, then death watch beetle, bark flaking off, a trunk

from which green twigs are growing. Straight up. No
grief, just a single-minded thought of light, light, light.

*

There is a forest in the forest.
Some might call it a clearing. But
sit still enough; see the sheer trunks of sunlight,
cross-hatched with dithering gnat-specks; hear
the quiver in the spreading boughs
of silence. The forest in the forest. And
the longer you sit, the grander it grows.

*

There is the big voice of the forest: wind
that floods, like a river not contained
to banks or gradient, a river that can wander,

that sinks away and reappears at will. Wind
leaning onto the tops, a long slow wave
that does not exhaust itself breaking.

And there is the small voice, never
quite exhausted either: bend, bend;
a few of us break but we bend.

There is the big voice, big wind rolling
here and there, whichever way it's marching.

And small voices, one here, one there,
not quite where you look or, when

you look, not there again.

*

Survivors. Leaf-litter, pine-litter, through the forest –
compacted on paths, more loosely under trees.
Near the edge of the village, it's piled.

People sweep the mulch-muck out of nearby gardens,
throw it back where it seems to belong.
I poke one with my stick, and it shows…

white. Touch it. Yes,
beneath an insulating crust of pine needles,
though it's June now, this is snow.

## A Monument in Vaikus

*Occupation Memorial, Maarjamäe, Tallinn*

A hillside

cleft. Dark wave
that rolls towards you

from the land (the Baltic
at your back is calmer), a wave

beneath which the craft you are is wrack.
is flotsam. Is consumed.

Or holds its course straight through
the scarp, the whelm, the null

of it. Makes for the sky
ahead. Stays true.

*

A wound. A sword slash
in the flesh of time, two walls
of glass-black marble,
facing,

and the narrowest way through.

A trench.
a tender and punctilious incision
like forensic archaeology.

*

Or
wings, raised above you,
the dark angel's, but

in remission, respite, restitution,
(you can count the years)
at rest, at least

for now.

*

This fault line in marble is both
the most eloquent speaking and scarcely
a speaking at all:
                                        the bare names,
twenty thousand, face each other
in plain equal font,
no voice raised louder than the other:
                                                            reticence
so any word you speak among them feels too much.

*

The impulse is to shout
and there's some power in that:

the back-and-forth echoes
endlessly according with each other,

till they too are a slab of polished black,
impervious to light, and no escape.

*

It's as dark as a mine.
Between the strata, prised painfully apart,
the names:

the most particular,
the rarest, most commonplace ore.

*

There is nothing unique, they say, about us,
this cross-section through unsaying.

There are countless others.

These deaths are merely our own.

*

This hill could slide closed,
the book of un-reading ever, as mute
to itself as fossils in un-split, unarticulated rock.

*

Some monuments are martial music
made of stone,
are march-pasts,
slowed, true, to a standstill
but still wearing their boots.

This, no: a hillside split by a shift
in the continent's edge – the way between,

a slow climb through the hillside
towards, though it is narrowed

to barely a hope,
a bare hope. Light. The sky.

Emerging there you find this state of inside
has an outside after all. A wall

of polished quietness. Apple trees,
new-planted. Four lines of a poem

and ten thousand silver, individual bees.

*

The murmur of a beehive is a synonym in sound
for silence,
                    not the kind that seals you in
but that which sets you free
to scribe your patterns on the air.

*

The bees are meant for homing, for
homecoming, but the light that catches them,

at distance, could be sparks
from a collapsing roof-tree or

an old man's bonfire (I could see
my father's silhouette against it)

in the night.

*

I can't conceive of music
it would be more right to sound here
than to stand
                        with not a note
played but the instruments held ready
listening
              and that is what I meant
to say. To write some bars
of that un-music
                          but in words.

*

No, of course, nothing, no name, no word, no stone
nor the most sincere treading out of paces,

can stand for the absences, take them away
from us (some of them, a grandfather,

other fragments of the family name,
will come with me, home)

and yet, speak carefully. Aim
for the word, the next one, not

right, ever. Just a shade less wrong.

## Five Versions of *Vaikus*

*valguse vaikus*

**A forest,** a real one –
I could give you day, time,
map location, the coordinates between

the chance of a clearing and a cloud
that, passing, sets a shape of light
amongst us,

sculptural.
A Standing Form
of silence. Centuries

of rusty spruce-mulch underfoot
and a catch in the wind's
breath,

urgent
as a heart beat
missed. A stillness in which if

a single thing falls, one dry needle
or this phenomenal
world,

it would be
(in a way that in this
life we never are) entirely heard.

*sipelgate vaikus*

**If it's the silence**

of the anthill's melée (like mass panic with a purpose)
that impresses you (the fire ants
piling their nest-tinder round the base of trees
as if for someone's burning at the stake)

re-tune your senses. On chemical

wavelengths, every bump-and-twiddle meeting, ant
to ant, is shouted conversation,
an order relayed. If we could hear the code
it would be pandemonium.

At most, we register a tang,

a pang of formic acid, rising from them like a city's
exhalation – almost soothing,
from a high enough perspective: a great body's
sweat, that work-worn, frantic, tireless,

timeless thing, the sigh of life.

*jänesekapsa vaikus*

**Aside**

at the path- or stream-side,
between lichen-haired stones, the corner
of whatever vision:
wood-sorrel. See
the way the shut books of its leaf-folds
tentatively open... or the implications
in its petals of pink-purple
that the nearly-
summer sky has, this far north,
just fringing it, at 2 am, that's both
the old day leaving and the new
already here...
or its slow lightening
to white with veins not quite too fine to see.

Wood sorrel:
leaf and flower nobody
thinks to eat till someone's fingertips
have confided a pinch to their hand,
someone they trust –
a taste
that's almost no taste – tart edge
to whatever walk or work has dulled in you,
whatever thirst
a little slaked,
whatever hunger just made clearer,
sourness touched
so lightly
it's a blessing. If the best
of silence could translate to taste

it tastes like this.

*hanede vaikus*

**Just when we thought**

that it could get no wider –
                                        the arm-
stretch of the day, the sky's late light
come down to earth, to sea,
                                        to linger
in it, way beyond its fading overhead,

and the broad shallow ripples that might
have begun from one duck's splash
a mile out
            oh, and the scope, the stillness…
When we thought we had it whole, then
this…
      With not so much sound
as a shudder of air, a ragged seam
of geese come low over the forest,
restitching themselves into flight,

to a wishbone, a wavering tick,
a not quite mended thread

that brings another out of no direction,
fragments of one gesture,
                                    to hitch
each to the other in a hundred-strong
single, first fluid then tightening vee,
not clamorous, not soundless, but

the grandest act of quiet
that casts itself
                        and us
into a distance where the *we*

who came to watch are out of sight.

It is complete.

*vaikimine*

**Learning to speak**

Estonian –
beginning with the silence… In words

I may not get beyond a scrap-bag
of vocabulary, the vowel sounds all askew

and no syntax to hold it.

But then,
by then, if I am fluent in the silence

I might already have got
where language works so hard to go.

## Another Shore

It's the job of the swifts this late July evening – the air almost too humid to cut through, but they do, the slim curved blades of dark they are, against its pink-grey... As we sit, words done for the day, they are shaving the edge of our silence, at the open windows, cutting level and low as if to make themselves particularly heard, each squeal-sweep stripping a sliver off what we are holding in this room. Not diminishing it. Rather, polishing the edges of the space with finer, finer abrasions. Like waves on a shore. They are making it clearer; cut glass or rock crystal come alive with points of light and dark inside... an inside which is just the world around it, all the outside focused inward. Concentrated. Now.

*

words

swift

edges

touch by touch

finessing

clarity